SPOTLIGHT ON GLOBAL ISSUES

THE **POVERTY** PROBLEM

Rachael Morlock

ROSEN PUBLISHING

NEW YORK

DISCARD

Published in 2022 by The Rosen Publishing Group, Inc.
29 East 21st Street, New York, NY 10010

Editor: Theresa Emminizer
Book Design: Michael Flynn

Photo Credits: Cover perfectlab/Shutterstock.com; (series globe background) photastic/Shutterstock.com; p. 4 Igor Alecsander/Getty Images; p. 5 N. Pipat/Shutterstock.com; p. 7 Arnold Sachs/Archive Photos/Getty Images; p. 8 Pongkiat Rungrojkarnka/EyeEm/Getty Images; p. 9 Mario Tama/Getty Images; p. 10 ssguy/Shutterstock.com; p. 11 Anton_Ivanov/Shutterstock.com; p. 12 Snehal Jeevan Pailkar/Shutterstock.com; p. 13 Tony Karumba/AFP/Getty Images; p. 15 NurPhoto/Getty Images; p. 16 Dmytro Zinkevych/Shutterstock.com; p. 17 Mike Kemp/In Pictures/Getty Images; p. 19 Ali Yussef/AFP/Getty Images; p. 20 Reg Speller/Hulton Archive/Getty Images; p. 21 Fotosearch/Archive Photos/Getty Images; p. 23 Bennett Raglin/Getty Images; p. 24 Gideon Mendel/Corbis Historical/Getty Images; p. 25 Mark Sagliocco/Getty Images; p. 26 Pallava Bagla/Corbis Historical/Getty Images; p. 27 PETIT Phillippe/Paris Match Archive/Getty Images; p. 29 Kevin Hagen/Getty Images.

Library of Congress Cataloging-in-Publication Data

Names: Morlock, Rachael, author.
Title: The poverty problem / Rachael Morlock.
Description: New York : Rosen Publishing, [2022] | Series: Spotlight on
   global issues | Includes index.
Identifiers: LCCN 2020007328 | ISBN 9781725323629 (library binding) | ISBN
   9781725323599 (paperback) | ISBN 9781725323605 (6 pack)
Subjects: LCSH: Poverty--Juvenile literature. | Social action--Juvenile
   literature. | Poverty--Measurement--Juvenile literature.
Classification: LCC HC79.P6 M6192 2022 | DDC 339.4/6--dc23
LC record available at https://lccn.loc.gov/2020007328

Manufactured in the United States of America

CPSIA Compliance Information: Batch #CSR22. For further information contact Rosen Publishing, New York, New York at 1-800-237-9932.

Find us on

CONTENTS

CHAPTER ONE

A GLOBAL
PROBLEM

How would you grow up to be strong and healthy if you didn't have enough to eat? What if you couldn't go to the doctor when you were sick? How successful would you be in school if you didn't have electricity? How would you light your house at night to study? How could you even go to school in the first place if your family needed you to help grow food or gather the water you needed to survive? These questions are daily concerns for people struggling with poverty.

For much of history, the majority of the world lived in extreme poverty like this. Daily activities were mainly focused on survival. This began to change about 200 years ago, after the Industrial Revolution. As work became more efficient, more people had the chance to rise out of extreme poverty. Attitudes toward poverty also changed over time.

In 2019, about 8 percent of the world population was living below the international poverty line.

In the last few centuries, the number of people living in extreme poverty has been falling. Today, extreme poverty means living on less than $1.90 a day. The World Bank has determined that this number represents the international poverty line. Over 600 million people live below this line around the world.

In 2015, the United Nations (UN) adopted a series of goals to guide the world toward safer, healthier, and more sustainable development. A top goal is to eliminate extreme poverty and reduce other forms of poverty by 2030. Creative solutions and thoughtful international policies are necessary to achieve this goal.

Is poverty a problem that can be solved? On a global level, poverty has seemed like a fact of life for most of history. Imagining a world without poverty would have been impossible until recently.

For centuries, people believed that poverty was inescapable. Many explained poverty by saying that some people deserved to be poor and that people's actions or choices kept them in poverty. Others explained poverty in terms of religion or fate. Economists and world leaders even believed that poverty was necessary in order to have a successful economy. They saw hunger as a way to make sure people would keep working.

New ideas about poverty began to develop in the late 18th century. Equality became an important ideal for philosophers and revolutionaries. They explored the benefits of promoting the welfare of all members of society. Around the same time, some people also became aware that the way society was organized created poverty. Institutions, not poor people, were responsible for poverty. Fighting poverty was part of good government.

In the 1960s, the poverty problem was given a surge of attention and energy. In the United States, the civil rights movement helped inspire President Lyndon B. Johnson's War on Poverty. The government directed policies at relieving the troubles of poor families.

This movement led to greater public awareness about global poverty. The idea that poverty was unacceptable was paired with a new hopefulness that it could be defeated. Today, the United Nations is committed to ending extreme poverty everywhere by 2030.

President Lyndon B. Johnson signed a bill meant to help fight poverty in 1964. The bill drew attention to inequalities in the United States.

CHAPTER TWO

MEASURES
OF POVERTY

Poverty can be measured in different ways. The international poverty line considers how much people consume every day around the world. Local currency and the cost of goods are part of this measurement. When measured in American money, this amount comes out to $1.90 a day.

In addition to the international poverty line, each country also has a national poverty line. This is specific to the living conditions and currency of each country. In the United States, the national poverty line is determined by income. For example, individuals who made less than $12,760 in 2020 fell below the poverty line.

Many people become stuck in relative poverty. If this lasts for several years, it's called persistent poverty. Long-term poverty has serious and negative effects on health and well-being.

Other ways of measuring poverty take into account absolute and relative poverty. Absolute measures assume that people everywhere have the same needs. Those needs include health care, basic education, food, shelter, access to clean water, sanitation, and access to information. According to the UN, people who lack at least two of these seven basic needs are living in absolute poverty. Measuring poverty this way makes it easier to observe and understand poverty around the world and over time.

Relative poverty takes more factors into consideration. It measures the poverty of individuals in comparison to other members of their society. It also takes into account specific aspects of their situation, location, and social relationships. In developed countries, more people live in relative poverty than absolute poverty. Their basic needs are met, but they have at least 50 percent less than average members of their society. This puts them at a disadvantage for accessing resources.

CHAPTER THREE

LOCATING
POVERTY

Poverty can be found all around the globe. In the past 30 years, the places in the world with the most poverty have changed significantly. The center of extreme poverty has shifted from east Asia to south Asia to sub-Saharan Africa.

In 1990, 1.9 billion people lived in extreme poverty. Over 1 billion people in this group were in China and India. Starting with China, major economic growth led to major changes. A strong economy included wider access to health care and education across the country. A similar trend followed in India. The economic growth and expanded social policies in these two countries meant that more than half of their poorest populations were no longer living in extreme poverty.

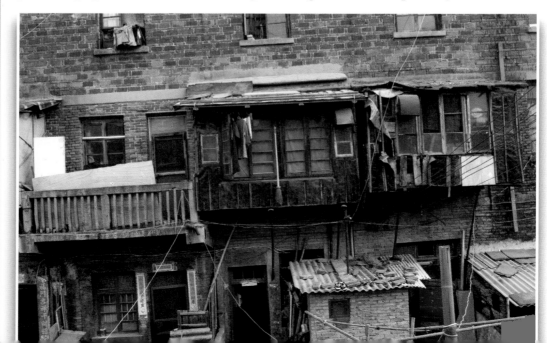

Although poverty has fallen around the world, it's risen in Africa. Madagascar is one of the poorest countries, with over three-fourths of the population living in extreme poverty.

In 2018, there were 650 million people living in extreme poverty. Most of them were in sub-Saharan Africa. Over half the population in the region lives in extreme poverty. Nigeria and the Democratic Republic of Congo have some of the highest levels of extreme poverty. National economic growth in these countries could have the same effect that it did in Asia, but positive change isn't guaranteed.

Without significant improvements, it's predicated that 500 million people will still be living in extreme poverty in 2030. An estimated 87 percent of that population will be in sub-Saharan Africa. In order to achieve the UN goal of eliminating extreme poverty worldwide by 2030, international efforts will need to focus on the particular needs of the poor in that region.

CHAPTER FOUR

WHAT CAUSES POVERTY?

The root causes of poverty are problems with resources. Healthy food, clean water, shelter, education, and health care are resources that support life. People without easy access to these resources often fall into poverty. Sometimes their access is restricted because resources aren't available where they live. Poverty is common in rural areas where the infrastructure needed to connect people with resources—including bridges, roads, and wells—is missing.

Social and political inequalities also cause poverty. Restrictions based on gender, class, and social standing can limit access to education and other necessities. Without an equal voice in community and government decisions, many people are unable to fight the forces that push them into poverty.

Social and economic barriers prevent many girls from attending school. Activist Malala Yousafzai, center, campaigns for the right to education. She has said, "Education is the best weapon we have to fight poverty, ignorance, and terrorism."

Reduced access to resources can also result from weather events related to climate change. Severe storms, dry spells, and floods can wipe out important resources, causing poverty around the world. These extreme events most heavily affect people who are already experiencing poverty.

Conflict and violence often lead directly to poverty. Large-scale conflicts such as wars and uprisings can destroy infrastructure and push people out of their homes and away from necessary resources. Everyday violence paired with ineffective law enforcement can also create conditions that limit access to important resources.

Without the basic necessities for life, it's impossible to leave behind the struggles of poverty. You'll often hear of the "cycle of poverty." That's because poverty is frequently passed down from one generation to the next. As a result, many social, political, and economic issues are both the cause and consequence of poverty.

Since childhood is such an important time for growth and development, experiencing extreme poverty at a young age is very damaging. In 2016, 385 million children were living in extreme poverty. Children living in poverty are more likely to become sick with diseases. In 2020, COVID-19 spread quickly all over the world. Not only did this increase the number of poor families in the world, it took an especially heavy toll on poor children everywhere. Reports say the pandemic forced at least 150 million children into poverty.

Women are also frequently affected by poverty. More women live in extreme poverty than men. On average, working women earn 24 percent less than men. Other women perform agricultural work or other work that's underpaid. Women are also often considered responsible for unpaid work such as childcare and household tasks. This limits income and can result in poverty. Single mothers are especially at risk.

Residents of rural settings are hit hard by poverty too. They often lack infrastructure and resources such as clean water, sanitation, and electricity. They're seven times more likely than city dwellers to drink contaminated, or dirty, water and to have to travel farther for safe water. People without clean, safe water are also more likely to become ill, miss work or school, and require health care.

People with disabilities form another group greatly affected by poverty. Disabilities prevent many from working. They lead to high health-care costs and poverty. Disabilities can also result from unsafe and unhealthy living conditions created by poverty.

More than 2 billion people don't have clean water at home. Instead, many girls and women must miss school, give up work, or put themselves in danger to find and carry water home.

CHAPTER FIVE

POVERTY
SOLUTIONS

The UN's sustainable development goal for reducing poverty is broken down into several targets for 2030. One step is to wipe out extreme poverty—measured in this case as $1.25 a day. Another target is to cut in half the number of people living below national poverty lines. The UN seeks to improve social systems that protect people from hardships, organize equal access to resources and services, and strengthen defenses against climate-related disasters. Efforts aim to support antipoverty programs in developing countries and assist national, regional, and international initiatives.

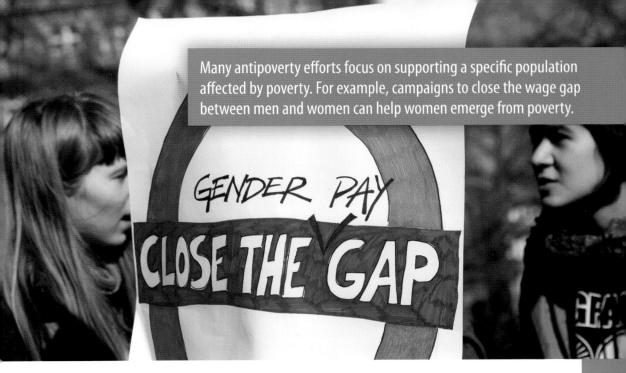

Many antipoverty efforts focus on supporting a specific population affected by poverty. For example, campaigns to close the wage gap between men and women can help women emerge from poverty.

GENDER PAY

CLOSE THE GAP

Many antipoverty initiatives fall into two groups. Some follow a top-down framework. This means that aid is provided to poor populations from outside their communities. This type of support is necessary when providing financial resources to communities with limited means. Many top-down solutions come from the state. They can take the form of infrastructure projects to build wells, improve roads, or expand transportation. The top-down approach often takes into account the big picture and can bring about short-term changes.

Other initiatives are bottom-up support. These antipoverty programs grow from within the affected communities. Making the most of local knowledge and connections, this kind of approach can be very specific to the concerns of a community. Bottom-up solutions focus on building skills and tools to make long-term improvements. Solving the poverty problem, whether from a bottom-up or top-down direction, begins with careful attention to the causes of poverty. Both approaches can make significant contributions to ending poverty.

The fight against poverty needs to focus on more than lifting people out of extreme poverty. It must also work on reducing inequality. In many countries, large gaps exist between income and opportunities for social classes.

Large inequality gaps aren't healthy for economies. Beyond that, inequality can lead to political and social unrest. It often means that the poorest members of society don't have the ability to realize their goals and achieve their greatest potential. Making sure that all members of society have access to resources and opportunities builds healthier nations and leads to more sustainable growth.

Economic growth in developing countries doesn't always help the poorest populations. In places with high inequality, a country can become wealthier and still have a high proportion of people living in poverty. In many countries, inequality has increased over the past 25 years.

It's common for the lowest 40 percent of workers in a nation to earn less than 25 percent of the overall income. At the same time, the top 1 percent of earners often control the majority of a country's wealth. The income of this top 1 percent is increasing in many countries.

To counter inequality, the World Bank promotes a policy of shared prosperity. This strategy focuses on supporting the poorest members of society with government reforms. Effective reforms include supporting young children with early childhood and nutrition services, providing universal health coverage, offering quality education to all, and building up infrastructure by improving roads and adding access to electricity.

Reducing inequality improves the chance that people who are born into poverty will be able to escape the cycle.

To fight global inequality, developing countries must be a priority. After World War II, it became more common for developed nations to offer resources to developing countries. This is known as foreign aid. It can take the form of goods, skills, or financial grants and loans. Countries provide foreign aid in order to help developing economies, assist in emergency situations such as natural disasters, build international relationships, avoid terrorism, and protect human rights around the world.

Three main international organizations work to support worldwide economic growth. These are the United Nations Development Program, the World Bank, and the International Monetary Fund. Foreign aid also comes from individual countries and from nongovernmental organizations (NGOs).

In 1949, President Harry Truman announced his goal of providing aid to "underdeveloped" foreign countries in his Four Point Speech.

The benefits of foreign aid for developing countries have been widely debated. Some argue it's a quick fix that keeps cycles of poverty intact. It's also criticized for interfering with economic growth. Opponents worry that foreign aid makes developing countries rely too much on the international community. They fear that it encourages government corruption.

Academic studies have tried to determine how much foreign aid helps developing nations. Although the benefits are often small, foreign aid usually does boost economic growth. These results may have been impossible otherwise.

Not all foreign aid should be measured in terms of its effects on the economy. Aid also improves the welfare of people living in poverty by focusing on services like health care or education. Some foreign aid fixes may be short term, but they can make a big difference for individuals in need of resources.

CHAPTER SIX

MICROFINANCING

Microfinancing can help people living in developing economies on a smaller scale than foreign aid. Economist Muhammad Yunus first developed the idea for microfinancing in Bangladesh in the 1970s.

Most people living in extreme poverty can't access financial tools such as traditional bank loans or credit. They don't have the resources necessary to prove their ability to pay back a loan. To solve this problem, Yunus and his bank began offering microloans. These loans are usually a few hundred dollars or less. They're paid back in small portions on a regular schedule, often weekly.

Microloans were originally intended to help people in poverty start small businesses. The loan supplied the extra money needed to begin a business. Loaners hoped that small businesses would bring in enough income to pull people out of poverty.

Now that microfinancing has been in use for several decades, there's more data available about its effectiveness. This shows that microloans aren't as helpful as expected in lifting individuals and families out of poverty. They're also only minimally effective in helping people in poverty start small, successful businesses.

However, microfinancing has still been an important tool. People living in extreme poverty have used microloans to cover emergency or unexpected expenses, such as health care or home repairs. They provide a necessary resource for people who are struggling to get by. Microloans can also offer people living in poverty a sense of choice and greater options when planning for the future.

Muhammad Yunus and his Grameen Bank were awarded the Nobel Peace Prize in 2006. Yunus's model of microfinancing began in Bangladesh, but it's spread to many developing countries.

WHITAKER
PEACE & DEVELOPMENT
INITIATIVE

CHAPTER SEVEN

CLIMATE PROTECTIONS

Climate change has negative effects around the world, especially for the most poor and vulnerable members of society. It's become faster and more extreme as the result of human activities that burn fossil fuels. Climate change takes form in rising global temperatures, rising sea levels, more frequent and intense storms, and increased air and water pollution.

When a cyclone, flood, or another extreme weather event affects an area, people living in poverty can't recover easily. Farmers lose their food source and livelihood. Many people lose their homes, have their water sources contaminated, or require health care after a disaster.

Every year, 26 million people are pushed into poverty by natural disasters. Many others are forced to migrate in search of better living conditions. It's predicted that there will be 143 million climate migrants by 2050.

Xiuhtezcatl Roske-Martinez became a climate activist at age six. As a teenager, he's addressed the UN and worked for Earth Guardians. He motivates other young people to protect the planet.

Protecting people in poverty means helping them prepare for the effects of climate change. The World Bank does this by helping communities build homes and infrastructure that can withstand natural disasters. People put early warning systems in place to alert communities about upcoming emergencies. For example, the World Bank has helped prepare the community for flooding after cyclones in the city of Beira, Mozambique.

No matter where you are in the world, your actions affect climate change. All countries can protect people in poverty by investing in renewable energy and curbing fossil fuel use. International action is required in order to avoid the worst effects of climate change, especially for the poorest members of society.

CHAPTER EIGHT

ENGINEERING SOLUTIONS

Technology has great potential for reducing poverty. It was technology that began the global shift away from poverty 200 years ago. The Industrial Revolution made work more efficient with new tools and technologies. Over time, workers began to rise out of poverty.

More recent technological developments offer alternatives to the fossil fuel–heavy industries of the past. Renewable energy is not only better for the environment, it can also radically change the lives of people living in poverty. Energy from solar, wind, and water sources can improve daily life without expensive power plants.

Solar power is used in many ways in poor or rural areas. Solar-powered cookstoves can eliminate the need for smoky fires in the home, improving air quality and health. Solar water pumps supply safe water after floods. Solar-powered computers can be used for online education in remote communities. Online classrooms make it easier for children and adults to gain an education, and education is one of the best tools for escaping poverty.

SOLAR WATER PUMP

Today, 840 million people live without electricity. In Morocco, people are building a giant solar power plant to provide energy to over 1 million people. Solar energy will help even more people as it becomes more efficient and less expensive.

People around the world are becoming more connected with mobile phones. Powerful wireless networks reach people in even the most remote locations. Having a mobile connection can help people living in poverty access banking services, health care, emergency alerts, and other important services and information.

Engineering solutions to reduce poverty are limitless. They can make a difference on every level of poverty reform. From supplying more effective agricultural tools to designing new public transportation systems, technology can provide tools and connections to lift people out of poverty.

New tools and technology can help reduce global poverty. So can social reforms and programs. One way to help people living in poverty is to make sure that fundamental services are available to everyone, regardless of their income.

A number of international, national, and nongovernmental organizations focus on making sure that people around the world have access to food, clean water, housing, health care, and other necessary services. You can play a part in tackling poverty by supporting or volunteering with one of these trusted organizations. You can also develop your own antipoverty projects.

Although extreme poverty is mostly found in developing countries, people all around the world have trouble accessing resources. Amika George became aware of one aspect of poverty in England, one of the wealthiest countries in the world. She learned that one in 10 girls in her country can't afford menstrual products. As a result, many miss school when they have their period.

This is another example of the way that poverty works in a cycle. Period poverty prevents girls from working or attending school. In turn, interruptions in work or school can push individuals further into poverty.

To combat period poverty, George worked to make menstrual products more available. When she was 17, George started #FreePeriods. The campaign grew from a small online petition to a large movement. With thousands of supporters and generous donations, #FreePeriods caught the attention of British lawmakers. In 2019, the government promised to provide free menstrual products in all secondary schools and colleges in England.

Amika George wants to make sure that girls have the supplies they need for their period. She has also tried to increase education and decrease embarrassment around periods.

CHAPTER NINE

SOLVING
THE PROBLEM

The UN adopted the Universal Declaration of Human Rights in 1948. The declaration sets out the basic rights of everyone in the world, no matter what their identity is or where they live. According to the declaration, everyone has a right to dignity and equality. They deserve the basic necessities of life—food, clothing, housing, medical care, and education.

People who live in extreme poverty are denied their human rights when they have to go without essentials. Many others live above the extreme poverty line but still can't access the resources they need to thrive. Poverty is a threat to human rights. That means that finding solutions to the poverty problem is a global responsibility.

Everyone can play a part in ending poverty. You can fight global poverty by supporting international organizations that help people in developing countries access basic resources. You can urge your government to provide aid to countries in need.

More locally, you can learn about the ways that poverty affects people in your community. Look for volunteer opportunities or fundraisers for local food banks or homeless shelters. They might be able to connect you with other services that help people living in poverty.

Urge your lawmakers to support policies that reduce inequality in your community, country, and the world. You can also take action on a personal, community, national, or international level to fight back against climate change. The 2030 goal of reducing poverty is possible if the global community works together.

GLOSSARY

activist (AK-tih-vist) Someone who acts strongly in support of or against an issue.

alternative (ol-TUHR-nuh-tiv) Something that can be chosen instead of something else.

corruption (kuh-RUHP-shuhn) Dishonest or illegal behavior, especially by powerful people.

dignity (DIG-nuh-tee) The quality or state of being worthy of respect.

economist (ih-KAH-nuh-mist) Someone who studies economics, or the system or process by which goods and services are made, sold, and bought in an area.

efficient (ih-FIH-suhnt) Done in the quickest and best way possible.

fossil fuel (FAH-suhl FYOOL) A fuel—such as coal, oil, or natural gas—that's formed in the earth from dead plants or animals.

Industrial Revolution (in-DUH-stree-uhl reh-vuh-LOO-shuhn) An era of social and economic changes marked by advances in technology and science.

infrastructure (IN-fruh-struhk-chuhr) The equipment and structures needed for a country, state, or region to function properly.

institution (in-stuh-TOO-shuhn) A custom, practice, or law that's accepted and used by many people.

menstrual (MEN-struh-uhl) Related to the periodic discharge of blood from females during menstruation.

nutrition (noo-TRIH-shuhn) The process of eating the right food to grow and be healthy.

potential (puh-TEN-shuhl) Promise.

sanitation (sa-nuh-TAY-shuhn) The process of keeping places free from dirt and disease.

sustainable (suh-STAY-nuh-buhl) Able to last a long time.

technology (tek-NAH-luh-jee) A method that uses science to solve problems and the tools used to solve those problems.

terrorism (TEHR-uhr-ih-zuhm) The act of using violence or fear to challenge an authority.

INDEX

PRIMARY SOURCE LIST

Page 7
President Lyndon B. Johnson holds up his "war on poverty" bill. Photograph. Arnold Sachs. August 20, 1964. Washington, D.C. Archive Photos via Getty Images.

Page 21
President Harry S. Truman sitting in White House library. Photograph. 1950. Washington, D.C. Archive Photos. Fotosearch via Getty Images.

Page 23
Muhammad Yunus. Photograph. Bennett Raglin. September 27, 2019. New York City. Getty Images Entertainment.

WEBSITES

Due to the changing nature of Internet links, Rosen Publishing has developed an online list of websites related to the subject of this book. This site is updated regularly. Please use this link to access the list: www.powerkidslinks.com/SOGI/poverty